THE
VALE OF RHEIDOL
RAILWAY

· A PAST and PRESENT COMPANION ·

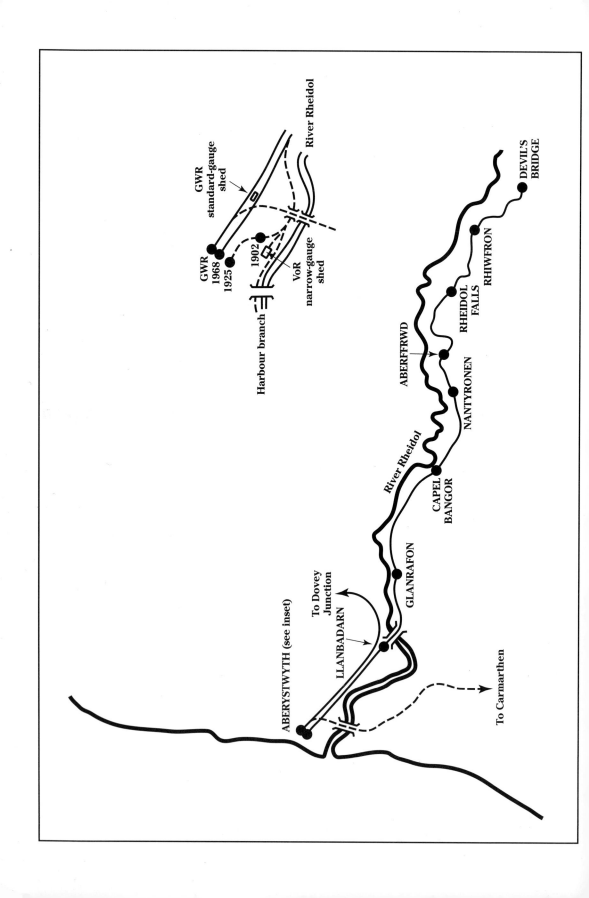

THE
VALE OF RHEIDOL
RAILWAY

• A PAST AND PRESENT COMPANION •

A nostalgic trip along the line from Aberystwyth to Devil's Bridge

Hugh Ballantyne

• RAILWAY HERITAGE •

from

The NOSTALGIA Collection

First published in 2003

British Library Cataloguing in Publication Data

A catalogue record for this book is available from the British Library.

ISBN 1 85895 155 0

Past & Present Publishing Ltd
The Trundle
Ringstead Road
Great Addington
Kettering
Northants NN14 4BW

Tel/Fax: 01536 330588
email: sales@nostalgiacollection.com
Website: www.nostalgiacollection.com

Printed and bound in Great Britain

Past and
Present

A Past & Present book
from
The **NOSTALGIA** *Collection*

ACKNOWLEDGEMENTS

This book has been prepared with the generous help and assistance of many people. I would particularly like to thank the Manager of the Vale of Rheidol Railway, Neil Thompson, who not only kindly gave me facilities to photograph and travel on the railway but also gave me his time to answer innumerable questions, and his staff, who were also most helpful and forthcoming. Outside the railway, my particular thanks go to John K. Williams of Blythe Bridge, Martin Smith, editor of *Railway Bylines*, and Geoffrey Dingle of Eccleshall for assistance and information. Numerous railway photographer colleagues also willingly offered me their work and they are credited, as appropriate, in the book. Last, but not least, I thank Madeleine Brown of Trentham, Stoke-on-Trent, who has typed all my notes and put the text on disk.

CONTENTS

BIBLIOGRAPHY

Boyd, J. I. C. *Narrow Gauge Rails in Mid Wales* (Oakwood Press)
Christiansen, R. and Miller, R.. W. *The Cambrian Railways* (David & Charles)
Cozens, Lewis *The Vale of Rheidol Railway* (Author)
Green, C. C. *The Vale of Rheidol Light Railway* (Wild Swan Publications Limited)
    The Cambrian Railways (Wild Swan Publications Limited)
Reeves, J. *Vale of Rheidol Railway Pictorial* (D. Bradford Barton Limited)

Magazines:
Railway Bylines
The Railway Magazine
The Railway Observer

In August 1967 No 9 *Prince of Wales* **is cleaned outside the shed at Aberystwyth prior to the day's work.** *Alan Wild*

INTRODUCTION

The origins of this railway were no less chequered in its gestation period than many other lines whose promoters' aspirations often ran ahead of reality or commercial prudence. Visitors to the beautiful area of the Rheidol Valley would be surprised to learn that in the latter part of the 19th century the population was nearly four times that of today, due to much lead-mining activity and timber estates coupled with foundries at Aberystwyth, which required transport to and from the mines. At that time Aberystwyth did not foresee a big future for tourists, although the railway was expected to help its development. Not surprisingly, due to the terrain the promoters decided on a 2-foot gauge railway (in fact built to 1ft 11½in), using the precedent of the Festiniog Railway. Following a Board of Trade enquiry held in Aberystwyth to resolve differences of opinion mainly regarding the harbour branch, the railway obtained its statutory powers in August 1897 by the Vale of Rheidol (Light) Railway Act 1897. Even so, there was difficulty for the promoters in raising the capital, and various amendments to the statutory provisions were required.

The contractors, Pethick Bros, started work in 1901 and the railway was opened for goods traffic on 15 August 1902, and passenger trains commenced on 22 December 1902. On 1 July 1913 the light railway was acquired by the Cambrian Railways, which in turn was absorbed, with a number of other Welsh railways, into the Great Western Railway on 25 March 1922. The GWR set about improving the condition of the track, locomotives and passenger stock, but goods traffic, which was feeling competition from road transport, ceased from 1 January 1927, and the regular year-round passenger services were also withdrawn after 31 December 1930. The GWR, being a highly publicity-conscious undertaking, successfully promoted the line as a seasonal tourist railway and it proved a popular attraction to visitors. When the Second World War was declared on 3 September 1939, the railway was closed at the end of that season and did not re-open until 23 July 1945.

All the main-line companies (and some minor railways) were nationalised by the Labour Government's Transport Act 1947, so on 1 January 1948 the railway became part of British Railways Western Region. Internal re-organisations within BR saw the Cambrian lines and the Vale of Rheidol transferred to the control of the London Midland Region, originally from Chester, and later in 1966 from Stoke-on-Trent.

Although it never made headline news, this little railway was the second part of the nationalised system to be sold to a private buyer. British Railways sold the Vale of Rheidol Railway Company Limited to the Brecon Mountain Railway on 31 March 1989, and in 1996 it was sold again to its present owners, the Phyllis Rampton Narrow-gauge Railway Trust. Today the railway is run by a highly motivated professional staff under its Manager, Neil Thompson, and, unlike most preserved railways, does not rely on volunteer staff.

Since BR days a considerable amount of maintenance arrears have been dealt with, including reconstruction of the Rheidol River Bridge, air-braking of locomotives and stock, complete relaying of the track, and acquisition of sections of forest alongside the line, so as to be able to open up the views into the valley where the railway thinks it is appropriate. For a century the railway has provided a wonderful journey with superb views as the steam-hauled train climbs up this lovely valley – long may it continue to do so.

Preserved locomotives stored on the railway for eventual museum display

Note: All are in derelict unserviceable condition as at August 2002

Type	No	Name	Builder	Original owner	Where stored
0-6-0T	6		John Fowler (10249/05)	Colonial Sugar Refining Co, Viti Levu, Fiji	Aberystwyth
0-4-2T	21		John Fowler (11938/09)	Sena Sugar Estates, Mozambique	Capel Bangor
0-6-2T	23		John Fowler (15515/20)	Sena Sugar Estates, Mozambique	Capel Bangor
0-4-0T			Decauville (1027/26)	Supplied to an industrial concern via agents in France	Aberystwyth
0-8-0T	968		Maffei (4766/16)	Heeresfeldbahn	Aberystwyth
0-4-0T/VB		*Kathleen*	De Winton, 1877	Penrhyn Slate Quarries	Aberystwyth
0-4-0ST		*Margaret*	Hunslet (605/94)	Penrhyn Slate Quarries	Aberystwyth (dismantled)

The Armorial Insignia on coach No 5, photographed on 31 August 1998. Incorporation of the railway was by means of the powers granted to the Light Railway Commissioners under the then new Light Railways Act 1896. *HB*

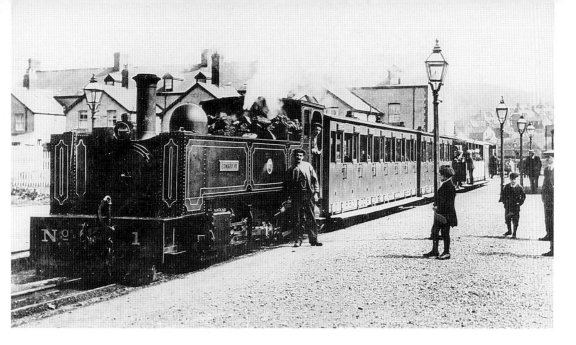

Aberystwyth passenger termini

A scene of activity at the original Aberystwyth terminus, which was situated at right angles to Park Avenue (then known as Smithfield Street). No 1 *Edward VII* is painted in a distinctive green livery with elaborate black and white lining. It is believed that the two 2-6-2Ts were repainted in this scheme from their original yellow livery in about 1909/10.

On 5 May 2002 the houses at the eastern end of Park Avenue are substantially the same. On the left is a row of houses in Maesyrafon with a low wall separating them from what had been the railway station, which is now the access road to the car park situated on the site of the original locomotive shed and sidings. *John K. Williams collection/HB*

These two well-known historic pictures also show trains in the original terminus. In the first, new 2-6-2T No 1 *Edward VII* stands with a rake of coaches, probably in the autumn/winter of 1902/1903. *John K. Williams collection*

The third engine of the original Vale of Rheidol stock was 2-4-0T *Rheidol* (Bagnall 1497/1896). Bought second-hand for the construction of the line, despite her small size she did useful work on the railway until withdrawn by the GWR in 1924. Here *Rheidol*, with her original spark-arresting chimney, blows off and is ready for departure from the original station with a lightweight train comprising one coach and one van in about 1903. *John K. Williams collection*

In 1925 the GWR extended the narrow-gauge line across Park Avenue, curving it westwards to be parallel to, but outside, the main standard-gauge terminus. A loop was constructed and passengers bought tickets and used the facilities of the main station, which was a much more convenient arrangement and better suited to attracting passengers. In this scene 2-6-2T No 8 stands on the curve towards Park Avenue on 7 July 1959 making ready to department with an afternoon train. The roofs of the main-line station are clearly visible behind the coaches.

Today the area south of the standard-gauge station is a car park, but the small building on the right of the earlier picture remains, and is the headquarters of the Aberystwyth Silver Band. *Terry Gough/HB*

This view is looking directly westwards (towards the sea) with the standard-gauge station visible on the right and Nos 9 and 8 getting ready to leave with the 1.45pm and 2.30pm trains to Devil's Bridge on an overcast summer's day, 6 August 1951.

This area is now part of a large car park, which is convenient for the standard-gauge station behind the wall and Somerfield's Supermarket on the left. *Both HB*

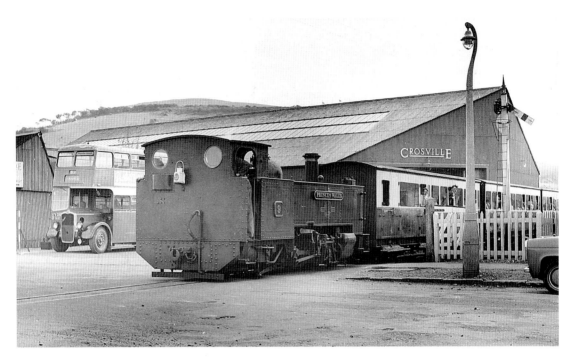

Coming across Park Avenue is No 9, bringing the 4.10pm train from Devil's Bridge into Aberystwyth station on 4 June 1963, the crossing being protected by the home signal on the right.

The Crosville bus depot remains virtually unaltered save for the name of the current operator, Arriva. Two small buses stand on what had been the trackbed behind the railings, and the road has been resurfaced and kerbed, leaving no trace of the narrow-gauge railway. *John Edgington/HB*

Inside the GWR station

Following the closure of the standard-gauge line from Aberystwyth to Carmarthen, the opportunity was eventually taken to replace that track in platforms 4 and 5, historically known as the 'Manchester & Milford bays', with narrow gauge rails, and the old line alongside the station and the level crossing at Park Avenue were done away with. From 20 May 1968 the narrow gauge was routed eastwards straight out of the station parallel to the standard gauge. This picture shows No 8 *Llywelyn* in Rail Blue livery with the BR white 'double arrow' logo beneath the nameplate, and the coaching stock also in blue, waiting to leave with the 2.30pm to Devil's Bridge on 26 April 1970.

By 5 May 1986 the lovely Great Western station has been sadly 'rationalised' (railway double-speak for official vandalism) by the removal of most of the platform awnings and platform 6's paving stones. No 8 is seen on its first day in the then new 'historic' livery of Cambrian 'invisible green' – to all intents and purposes looking like black – with the company name 'Cambrian' in 7-inch high letters on the tank sides, painted grey and shaded red. The coaches have also been repainted in the tasteful chocolate and cream livery of the GWR. This coincided with a Spring Gala Day and the train is the 14.20 to Devil's Bridge. *P. J. Lynch/HB*

On the same day as the previous picture, No 7 *Owain Glyndwr* in its 'historical' BR Western Region lined green livery, the painting of which had been sponsored by Shell-UK Limited (see page 63) is about to leave with the 10.30am train to Devil's Bridge, the first of five trains booked to run on this Spring Gala Day, necessitating the use of all three engines.

Twelve years later, in August 1998, the Somerfield Supermarket is well-established; the outside station wall and end awning have finally been removed and the narrow-gauge track-level platform re-tarmacked. No 8 is still green but unlined, lettered 'Great Western', the nameplate removed, and its two-line air pump equipment prominent on the front buffer-beam. The train is the 2.00pm to Devil's Bridge. *Both HB*

17

The original locomotive shed

This was the engine shed layout used from opening in 1902 until 1968, photographed on 4 June 1963. The original loco shed is the building immediately behind No 9, while the second building was first used as the fitters' shed. The space to the left of the water tank was part of the route of the Harbour Branch, used to bring some construction materials conveyed by sea, which ran alongside the wall and under the road bridge as a single line to end up on the Stone Quay, a distance of about 700 yards. This short branch was never viable and the track was lifted about 1930. *John Edgington*

In early BR days No 9 stands over the ash-pit outside the shed on 6 August 1951. Alongside is one of six wagons bought by the Rheidol Company from the Midland Carriage & Wagon Co Ltd in 1906, being used for loco coal, which was transhipped from the transfer siding near milepost ¾ (see page 26). All trace of that siding, and indeed the standard-gauge sidings in the area, have now been completed obliterated. *HB*

In August 1967, during the last year that the old shed was in use, No 9 *Prince of Wales* stands alongside some coal wagons. The one nearest the camera is one of the 'ex-Hafan' open wagons, originally one of a batch built by the Midland Carriage & Wagon Co in 1900 for the Plynlimon & Hafan Railway, but sold direct by the builders in 1901 to the Rheidol Company, due to the Hafan Co's liquidation (see also page 58).

The present scene is now a Council pay-and-display car park. The houses in Greenfield Street, in the right background, and Riverside Terrace, behind the loco shed, remain, as does the road bridge over the river. The other alteration has been the removal of the stone wall between the railway and the river, and its replacement by banking with a walkway along the top, built in connection with the Aberystwyth Tidal Defence Project. *Alan Wild/HB*

Just beyond the loco shed the railway came around the back of the bus garage and turned alongside the river before passing beneath the GWR line to Carmarthen. This view shows the river beyond the retaining wall and the engine shed in the distance, as No 7, still in GWR unlined green livery, heads a morning train to Devil's Bridge on 22 June 1953.

The present scene shows once again that the old stone wall has been replaced by a wide river-side bank topped with a footpath and railings as part of the Aberystwyth Tidal Defence Project. *P. J. Lynch/HB*

The standard-gauge shed

The former GWR standard-gauge shed, built in 1938 and closed to steam in April 1965, has been used by the Rheidol since 1968, which improved the amenities for staff working on the locomotives and coaching stock. It now contains three tracks, two of which extend out of the rear of the building. No 7 *Owain Glyndwr* approaches Aberystwyth station on 17 July 1990, while on the right is the derelict standard-gauge coal-stage topped by a water tank. *Terry Gough*

On 23 July 1988 at the back or eastern end of the present loco/carriage stock shed are some timber and open wagons. The banking and disused coal-stage/water tank is on the left, with the new running line opened in 1968 in front of it.

One could be forgiven for thinking that the Rheidol railway had closed when looking at this present-day picture! It is a fact of all railways that some stock is either awaiting repair or scrap and has to be stored somewhere – in this case outside the back of the loco/carriage shed. Despite appearances, these coaches may be overhauled, and the point sections are available for re-use if required. Notice that the coal stage and embankment in the past picture have been demolished and removed, and it is intended that a new station will be constructed in this area to replace the existing one at some future date. *Terry Gough/HB*

A lovely vintage picture of Aberystwyth shed in early BR days with three engines that epitomised secondary passenger services over much of the former Cambrian section at the time. Three '90XX' Class 4-4-0s, 1930s rebuilds from 'Dukes' and 'Bulldogs', and nicknamed 'Dukedogs'. Nos 9027, 9017 (now preserved on the Bluebell Railway) and 9021, are seen on a warm summer's day, 17 July 1955, awaiting their next turn of duty. They are standing where the current Vale of Rheidol running line out of Aberystwyth is now located. *Brian Moone*

'Dukedog' No 9005 stands alongside Aberystwyth shed, also on 17 July 1955. This engine was rebuilt in September 1936 as No 3205 with the frames from 'Bulldog' No 3413 *James Mason*, replacing 'Duke' No 3255 *Excalibur* and, for a short period, carrying the name *Earl of Devon*. It was renumbered 9005 in July 1946 and withdrawn in July 1959.

Today the smoke vents have been removed from the shed roof and No 9 *Prince of Wales* faces east, as the Rheidol engines have always done. Unlike No 9005 above, which could be turned at Aberystwyth, the Rheidol has no turning facilities. *Brian Moone/HB*

The interior of the former GWR engine shed on 5 May 1986, now used by the Rheidol for its locomotives and storage of stock. Nos 7 and 8 stand on the centre track of the three, and behind No 8 can be seen the hoist situated over the left-side track. *HB*

This was the exchange siding put in by the GWR in 1925 to replace a similar siding built by the Cambrian Railways in 1903; the narrow-gauge track interlaced with the standard gauge towards the Aberystwyth end. This 3 June 1963 photograph gives a good impression of the different scales and sizes of the coal wagons on the two gauges. The facing point mechanism was by Saxby & Farmer, and worked the running point and the single-bladed trap on the siding. The siding was closed and removed in 1968, and today no trace remains of either siding; as the Rheidol locomotives are oil-burners, oil fuel is delivered by lorry to the supply tank adjacent to the loco shed. *John Edgington*

A journey up the valley

The first stopping place on the journey to Devil's Bridge is Llanbadarn. Originally designated a station, it was never manned and, although it once had a waiting shelter, this has now been removed. Trains rarely pick up passengers here, but have to stop a few yards beyond the 'station' as the level crossing, once a rural lane, has now become a busy by-pass road. No 7 *Owain Glyndwr* is passing the station on an overcast 17 July 1963 en route to Devil's Bridge.

Nearly 40 years later, on 5 May 2002, No 9 *Prince of Wales* passes the same location. A replacement nameboard has been provided, while on the left the decrepit building has gone and the land tidied up to form a playground and sports field. *P. J. Lynch/HB*

In the Rail Blue era, on 2 June 1968, No 9 *Prince of Wales* pulls away from the level crossing stop at Llanbadarn and is heading on straight track towards the River Rheidol Bridge with the 2.15pm train from Aberystwyth.

Thirty years later, on 1 September 1998, the same engine, now in maroon livery and its coaches painted chocolate and cream, is heading the 12.15 train from Aberystwyth. Development on each side of the railway embankment, now much more overgrown, is confined to sports fields rather than building construction, although the boundary fence seems excessive in the circumstances. *Both HB*

By far the most important and largest bridge is a quarter of a mile beyond Llanbadarn where the railway crosses the River Rheidol on a substantial structure 113 feet long resting on six wooden trestle piers driven into the shingle bed of the river. No 9 is coming over the bridge with a Devil's Bridge-bound train on 17 July 1963.

Thirty-five years later, in August 1998, the same engine, now painted maroon, oil-fired and air-braked, crosses the bridge, which was rebuilt in the winter of 1991/92 with five trestles and fitted with metal hand-rails in place of the post-and-wire fencing. *P. J. Lynch/HB*

Another view of the Rheidol Bridge, taken on 2 June 1968, with No 9 *Prince of Wales* returning to Aberystwyth with the 4.45pm from Devil's Bridge. This picture shows the broad flood plain of the Rheidol in its lower reaches with the hills forming the southern side of the Vale, which the railway has to ascend, closing in towards Capel Bangor. Today, in addition to the rebuilt bridge, there is a substantial footbridge parallel to the right and a new gated foot crossing over the track in place of the stile. *HB*

Some 2 miles out of Aberystwyth an industrial estate has been developed at Glanrafon, just south of the main A44 road, and what had once just been an unprotected level crossing on a minor road has now become a mandatory stop for all trains. The crossing is protected by automatic flashing lights, and on 16 August 1987 No 9 *Prince of Wales*, in its historic original Vale of Rheidol yellow livery, cautiously approaches the crossing with the 10.30am train from Aberystwyth, at the time entitled – not very originally, it must be said – 'The Welsh Dragon'. *HB*

From Glanrafon towards Capel Bangor there is a mile-long straight section past milepost 3 (near which a station for a Territorial Army camp at Lovesgrove was located before the Great War) before the line curves into Capel Bangor station, 4½ miles from Aberystwyth. Originally a loop, siding, carriage shed and small corrugated steel station building were provided, but in 1962 the carriage shed, by then dilapidated, was sold to a farmer for its materials. The following year the loop and siding had gone, but by the time of this picture, 17 July 1990, a replacement local stone-built shelter had been provided. In high summer, amidst prolific weeds and grass, No 7 passes the station with the 12.15 from Aberystwyth.

To the great credit of the current management of the railway, Capel Bangor has been transformed, with the loop and siding re-instated and a nameboard with fencing on each side. Just visible at the end of the siding at the

west end of the station are a stored unserviceable coach and two Fowler-built tank engines from the Phyllis Rampton Narrow-gauge Trust, pending restoration and display at a future date in the proposed Narrow Gauge Museum (see page 8 for details of these locomotives). *Terry Gough/HB*

Above On passing the level crossing at the east end of Capel Bangor station, the railway curves towards the hillsides, and the gradients begin to steepen noticeably. On 19 June 1983 No 7 *Owain Glyndwr*, just re-commissioned after being repainted in BR lined green livery by its sponsors, Shell Oil (UK) Limited, is tackling the climb at the head of the 13.45 special working from Aberystwyth. In the background is a minor road bridge connecting the farms on the south side of the river with the larger settlement of Capel Bangor near the main A44 road. *HB*

Below Once past Capel Bangor climbing starts in earnest, and here, near the 6¼ milepost, it is 1 in 40 against the train and some 400 yards to go before the Nantyronen stop. No 8, in Great Western livery, is working the 14.00 from Aberystwyth on 1 September 1988. *HB*

The track levels off just before the level crossing on the run into Nantyronen station, and on 23 July 1988 the driver is keeping a sharp lookout as No 7 *Owain Glyndur* comes over the road. *Terry Gough*

Inset **The station nameboard on 31 August 1998.** *HB*

At one time Nantyronen had a siding and a waiting shelter; the former has long since been removed and the shelter replaced by a gangers' hut, which in turn was replaced by the one visible here behind the water tank on 5 May 1986. The water tank is also of interest as it was brought from Bold Colliery in 1982 where it had been used during May 1980 by the locomotives taking part in the Rainhill Cavalcade. No 8, in its Cambrian black livery, has just arrived with the 14.20 from Aberystwyth and is about to have its tanks topped up. *HB*

35

On 5 May 1986 the same train as in the previous photograph leaves Nantyronen to resume the 1 in 40 climb towards the next stop nearly a mile up the valley at Aberffrwd. *HB*

Above Aberffrwd, 7½ miles from Aberystwyth, was used until 1982 as the intermediate water stop and loop for crossing trains. In the earliest days of the railway a station was opened on 27 April 1904, complete with loop and signals. The location is cut into the steep hillside so that the little station building needed rear support for its overhang and the water tanks had to be recessed into the hillside. This July 1960 picture shows the water column at the Aberystwyth end, the loop line on the right and the signal posts with their arms removed. *Terry Gough*

Below Twelve years later, on 8 August 1972, No 9 *Prince of Wales*, in Rail Blue livery, is taking water from the column at the Devil's Bridge end of the station. The loop line was removed in 1963, the water column repositioned and the station later demolished. *J. H. Aston, John K. Williams collection*

The 'past' picture was taken in July 1960 on the same occasion as the upper one on the previous page, but from a different angle, while the 'present' view, repeated 42 years later, shows the same engine arriving with the 11.00 train from Aberystwyth. The ground frame for the points at the western end of the re-laid loop stands where the water column used to be. The loop, re-instated in 1990, was slightly extended, and round the bend out of sight is a new up home signal. *Terry Gough/HB*

From Aberffrwd it is a continuous slog at 1 in 50 for 4 miles to just short of the terminus. There are no more stations, but the view through the gaps in the trees and the series of curves around the hillsides make for a memorable journey. Near milepost 9¼ there is a halt at Rheidol Falls. This well-known picture shows a downhill mixed train at the halt in about 1926.

It is impossible to repeat the above picture due to dense vegetation on the hillsides, and passengers today are unaware of the view outwards into the valley due to the trees growing high above rail level on the downward slope. However, the railway has more recently been able to purchase parcels of woodland bordering the line and is embarking on a programme of opening up the views where possible. *John K. Williams collection/HB*

Above No 8, in Great Western livery, runs along the ledge about 430 feet above sea level just beyond Rheidol Falls halt. In the bottom of the valley is the river, and the footbridge over the falls can just be seen, while on the opposite side of the valley is the scar of old mine workings that, because of its shape, is known as 'the stag'. The train is the 10.45 from Aberystwyth on 1 September 1998. *HB*

Below A few yards further up the hill the railway goes round a rock face on yet another sharp curve on well-laid track protected by a check rail. Affixed to the rock is a commemorative tablet to Oliver Veltom, a railwayman who had much regard for this little railway, and whose ashes were scattered here in 1980. *HB*

Above The unbroken climb at 1 in 50, studded with reverse curves, continues past Rhiwfron almost into Devil's Bridge station. In this section there are traces of several derelict lead and zinc ore mines, of which the principal were the Cwmrheidol and Erwtomau, but all were worked out by 1925. These four pictures, taken in three of the four eras of the railway – the early years, the GWR period, and under BR ownership – show trains on these upper sections of the railway. The first is a well-known commercial postcard of one of the original 2-6-2Ts near Quarry Cutting. This particular card, published in the Frank Phillips series, Aberystwyth, was posted from Aberystwyth on 19 August 1913 to a Miss Brocklehurst at Whaley Bridge, postage ½d! *John K. Williams collection*

Below This even older scene, but on a more modern postcard, shows Bagnall 2-4-0T No 3 *Rheidol* in the same area, the postcard being an F. Frith, Reigate, issue, but posted from Southall to Ipswich in December 1960! *John K. Williams collection*

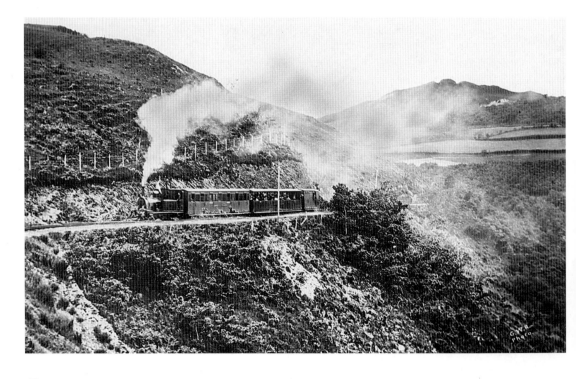

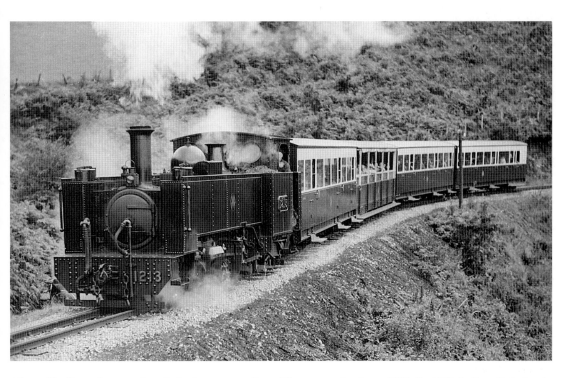

Above Hauling a four-coach train in the pre-war Great Western era in about 1938, No 1213, built at Swindon in 1924 (later renumbered 9) and carrying the GWR roundel emblem on the tank side, is working hard on the reverse curves and 1 in 50 gradient. *John K. Williams collection*

Below Here is No 9 again, but this time in about 1952, in the early BR era when the coaching stock was painted in red and cream livery. This card, published by Harvey Barton & Son Limited, Bristol, is obviously a posed scene with the open door and the passenger outside the third carriage. *John K. Williams collection*

DEVIL'S BRIDGE TRAIN VALE OF RHEIDOL RAILWAY   57016

Climbing hard on the hillside east of Rhiwfron way above the river, No 8 *Llywelyn*, in GWR unlined green livery, is hauling a train of stock newly repainted in GWR chocolate and cream livery, forming the 14.10 service from Aberystwyth on 2 May 1983. *HB*

Very near Devil's Bridge there is a last reverse curve before the train enters Quarry Cutting, where No 8 is seen working the 2.00pm train from Aberystwyth on 6 August 1951.

The same engine, now lettered 'Great Western' in full on its tank sides, oil-burning and with its two-line air-pump prominent, is seen at the same location 47 years later, showing much more lineside vegetation on both sides of the track. *Both HB*

This is the sharp curve at 1 in 50 through Quarry Cutting, well above the 600-foot contour, looking towards Devil's Bridge on 6 August 1951. *HB*

A striking picture of No 9 blasting around the tight curve through Quarry Cutting with the 10.40 from Aberystwyth on 8 August 1973. *Roger Siviter*

Above Finally, after the long climb up the southern side of the Rheidol Valley, the railway reaches its terminus at Devil's Bridge, just under 12 miles from Aberystwyth. This early postcard view, looking west and believed to have been taken in about 1905, shows 2-4-0T *Rheidol* on arrival with its lightweight train. Note the neat layout and the station building in corrugated steel sheeting flanked by some elegant lamp-posts. *John K. Williams collection*

Below Looking in the opposite direction, also in about 1905, we see another train and the goods yard in the background. Visible is a pony and trap, a timber bolster wagon and some open wagons. Protruding over the station roof is the jib of the derrick crane that was removed in 1919. *John K. Williams collection*

These two pictures show subtle changes in the Devil's Bridge layout in the early BR era. Visible are two sidings to the left of the goods shed, which clearly looks out of use and dilapidated, and a third short siding upon which is one of the three neat little guard's vans and an open wagon. No 9 is buffered up to its train ready for the return journey to Aberystwyth on 17 July 1955.

Eight years later John Edgington returned to Devil's Bridge, by which time the goods shed had been demolished and the vegetation on the south-side embankment was getting thicker. No 9 is again waiting to leave with the 4.30pm back to Aberystwyth on 2 June 1963. *Both John Edgington*

Looking from the buffer stops, No 8, in early BR livery, has arrived on a warm summer's day, 17 July 1955. Almost half a century later, on 5 May 2002, the station building remains the same, and other than livery changes to the locomotive and train, together with the air-pump on the buffer-beam of No 9, the scene has not altered much. The track has heavier rail and the check rails on the points are shorter. *John Edgington/HB*

Today there is only one siding at Devil's Bridge, and the former goods yard is given over to car parking together with a refreshment-hut-cum-sales-shop. No 9, not visible because of the overhanging vegetation, has just arrived with the 11.00 from Aberystwyth on 5 May 2002. *HB*

Above left After running round its train upon arrival, the engine goes to the water column situated just outside the facing points into the station loop. This time-honoured event was once seen to good advantage from the top of the deep cutting accessed from the minor road overbridge. When this picture was taken, on 17 July 1955, there was still a home signal adjacent to the water tank to protect the station. No 8 is taking water. *John Edgington*

Left No 9, repainted in the distinctive original Vale of Rheidol yellow livery, takes water on 2 May 1983. Today it is impossible to get a photograph from this angle due to the dense undergrowth on the cutting side and top, but as all engines continue to be watered here before their return to Aberystwyth, the only position is head on from the occupation road bridge (which is the only bridge over the railway). *HB*

Above The bi-lingual station nameboard. The height above sea level is contentious – some authorities state that the station is 680 feet above sea level! Irrespective of this, the author's wife has enjoyed the train ride up the valley on 29 August 1998! *HB*

The Davies & Metcalfe tanks

The Vale of Rheidol's original pair of 2-6-2T's were supplied by Davies & Metcalfe Ltd of Romily near Manchester to the design of William Szlumper – somewhat similar to the existing Lynton & Barnstaple 2-6-2Ts – and were delivered to the Vale of Rheidol in 1902. On arrival at Aberystwyth the locomotives were in works grey, but were quickly painted yellow in the style of the London, Brighton & South Coast Railway. This picture of No 1 *Edward VII* taken at the original Aberystwyth station on 28 June 1909 does not clearly show the bright livery of the engine. *LCGB, Ken Nunn Collection*

The second Davies & Metcalfe 2-6-2T, No 2 *Prince of Wales*, is seen at Aberystwyth on 30 June 1909, but repainted green with elaborate darker green and black lining around the tank sides and contours of the cab. No 1 was also repainted in this livery some time about 1909/10. Note that both engines as built had the cab sides flush with the tanks, so that there was no space for coal other than piled on top of the firebox in front of the cab, as seen here. This engine went to Swindon for repairs in 1924, but was withdrawn from service. *LCGB, Ken Nunn Collection*

When the Vale of Rheidol was acquired by the Cambrian Railways in 1913, the 2-6-2Ts lost their names and green livery. No 1 is seen here in plain black livery with the company name 'Cambrian', in 7-inch-high letters painted grey and edged in red, on the tank sides. At about this time, as can be seen, the cab sides were widened to allow more bunker space for coal. Also, a half-drum protrusion in the cab back sheet allowed the handbrake to turn full circle, and to be repositioned for easier use. This picture of No 1, with 2-4-0T *Rheidol*, was taken at Devil's Bridge in about 1921. *Great Western Trust, W. L. Good collection*

This photograph shows No 1 in Great Western livery as No 1212, and was taken at Swindon some time between 1932, when she was stored as surplus to requirements, with three modern successors to work the line, and March 1935, when she was scrapped. *John K. Williams collection*

Bagnall 2-4-0T No 3 *Rheidol*

Below This engine was built by W. G. Bagnall & Co Ltd of Stafford in 1896, works number 1497, to the order of a sugar factory in Brazil, Usina Troze de Maio (Portuguese for '13 May'), but the order was cancelled due to disorder in the country at the time. In August 1897 it was bought to work on the Plynlimon & Hafan Tramway, re-gauged from 75cm to 2ft 3in and named *Talybont*. Following the closure of the P & H Tramway, Bagnall bought back the loco and re-gauged it again to 1ft 11½in for the use of the contractors building the Vale of Rheidol, Pethick Bros of Plymouth. In 1902 the contractors sold the engine to the Vale of Rheidol Company, which thought it would be useful for shunting and working the Aberystwyth Harbour branch. In fact, the locomotive had a hard life and frequently worked trains up to Devil's Bridge. This picture, taken in about 1908 at Aberystwyth, shows *Rheidol* in lined green livery with the name painted on the side tank. *John K. Williams collection*

Bottom No 3 is standing outside Aberystwyth shed in about 1921, and by now has lost its name, which has been substituted by the words 'Cambrian Railways'. The wooden rear of the cab has been replaced by sheet metal and the front buffer has been cut away at the lower corners to give better access to the cylinder heads. Shortly after the Cambrian was absorbed into the Great Western in 1922, No 3 was allocated the number 1198, but never carried it as the engine was stopped on 31 May 1923 and officially withdrawn in July 1924. *Great Western Trust collection*

The Swindon-built tanks

Above The Great Western Railway found that it had inherited one small worn-out 2-4-0T, and the two 2-6-2Ts, although of sound design, were badly in need of overhaul to GWR standards. Authority was obtained under Lot 227 for two new 2-6-2Ts similar in appearance to Nos 1 and 2, but with Belpaire fireboxes, a heavier set of Walschaerts valve-gear and more coal capacity, so increasing the weight by 3 tons compared with the originals. Boiler pressure was also increased from 150 to 165psi, which produced a 20 per cent increase in tractive effort to 10,150lb. The official completion date was 19 October 1923, and the cost was £2,737 each. Except for livery and naming, and the much later adaptation for oil-firing and the fitting of the two-line air-pumps, their appearance has remained very much as built. This picture shows No 7 on 4 May 1981 painted in BR Corporate blue lined in black and white, named *Owain Glyndwr* with a red background to the nameplate, and with a raised brass BR 'double arrow' emblem on the cabside. *John K. Williams collection*

Below No 8 *Llywelyn*, in BR unlined blue, a red background to the nameplate, and a white-painted BR 'double arrow' emblem, is seen at Devil's Bridge on 26 April 1970. *P. J. Lynch*

This engine had an interesting birth! 1213 was the GWR number allocated to Vale of Rheidol No 2, which officially went to Swindon for overhaul in 1924. However, as has now been established, the engine that emerged – as No 1213 – was in fact a completely new locomotive with the same features and improvements as the two new 2-6-2Ts before it, Nos 7 and 8. It is thought that for accounting purposes the third new engine was shown in the Works records as a rebuilding, but in fact the original No 2 was scrapped at about this time. Here the 1924-built No 1213 stands at Aberystwyth with a Devil's Bridge train in GWR unlined green with the GWR circular totem, which it received in 1936. The photograph was taken between 1936 and 1938, during the time that the prominent steam-heating pipes were attached to the front buffer-beam. *John K. Williams collection*

During the winter of 1948/49 No 1213 was painted plain black and renumbered 9. This picture shows the locomotive, named *Prince of Wales* and painted in BR unlined Corporate blue with a red background to the name and numberplates, on 24 April 1970. *P. J. Lynch*

61

No 8 undergoing overhaul in 'A' Shop at Swindon on 26 May 1954. *HB*

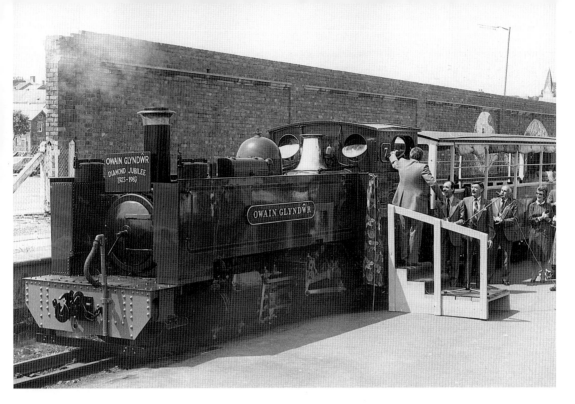

Above A celebration to mark the return of historical liveries took place in the early 1980s, and the Diamond Jubilee of No 7 *Owain Glyndwr* saw a re-commissioning ceremony (the engine having been converted to oil-firing in 1978) sponsored by Shell Oil (UK) Limited, with the engine repainted in BR lined green livery. This picture shows the ceremony at Aberystwyth on 19 June 1983 being performed by Mr R. Vaughan of Shell, watched by Mr E. A. Gibbins, the BR Divisional Manager, and Messrs Rowlands and Jones, Mayor of Aberystwyth and Chairman of Ceredigion District Council respectively. *HB*

Below In spotless condition, No 7 and its train of chocolate and cream coaches enters Devil's Bridge station with the 14.00 service from Aberystwyth on 5 May 1986. *HB*

Above This is No 9 in its present striking maroon livery, lined in black and yellow, with polished brass and copper, all in spotless condition. It is the practice of the present management to allow the engine arriving at Devil's Bridge to detach from its train, move forward to the buffer stop in the headshunt and stay there until it is time to run back past its train to the water tank to take water and re-attach to the downhill train. This enables members of the public to admire the engine and take unhurried pictures of it, similar to this 29 August 1998 view. *HB*

Below The maker's plate attached to the cab side sheets of No 9. *HB*

The two 1923 Swindon-built 2-6-2Ts stand outside the former standard-gauge shed at Aberystwyth on 13 September 1986. No 7 is in BR lined green livery (except that it has '7' painted on the buffer-beam instead of a smokebox-door numberplate) and No 8 is in Cambrian 'invisible green' – appearing black – with 'Cambrian' on the tank sides. No 7 was converted to oil-firing in 1978 and fitted with a two-line air-braking system in 1992. No 8 was converted to oil-firing in 1979, and the air-brake was fitted in 1996. *HB*

Reflections of No 9's bright yellow livery as the locomotive is prepared outside Aberystwyth shed – in the rain – for the Spring Gala Day on 2 May 1983. No 9 was converted to oil-firing in 1981, and was the first of the trio to be air-braked, in 1991. *HB*

Non-steam motive power

In 1988 BR bought this Bagguley Drewry-type 0-6-0 diesel, built to order by the Brecon Mountain Railway in 1987. It is a very useful locomotive and in regular use today for shunting and for use on PW trains, etc. It was, quite logically, numbered 10, and given a GWR-style numberplate attached to the cabside. It is seen at Aberystwyth station on 5 August 1988. *HB*

Above The railway has a Permaquip diesel-hydraulic Personnel Carrier used for PW and other maintenance work. *HB*

Below A most valuable and useful piece of equipment is this Plasser rail tamping machine. It was built in 1985 for use in a South African gold mine, but Plasser brought it back, reconditioned it in 1991 and sold it to the Vale of Rheidol. *HB*

Wickham trolley TR26 was powered by a twin-cylinder JAP air-cooled engine and was cut down to 1ft 11½in gauge at Wolverhampton Works in 1963. Here it is being placed on the running line by Aberystwyth loco shed just after the 10.30 train to Devil's Bridge had departed in August 1967. It was withdrawn in 1984 and replaced in 1985 by the Permaquip seen opposite. *Alan Wild*

Visiting locomotives

Above In the summer of 1912 the Territorial Army opened a camp at Lovesgrove, just over 3¼ miles from Aberystwyth, and another at Devil's Bridge, so the surge in traffic caused an immediate motive power problem for the railway. The Festiniog Railway was approached, and it agreed to hire to the Vale of Rheidol its 0-4-0ST *Palmerston* (built by George England in 1864). It worked on the line quite successfully for three weeks in August 1912 at a charge of £2 per day, which included the services of its regular driver, David Davies – apparently a 'character' who loved his engine so much that he slept in the tender at night so as to guard it against the Rheidol men! (Did his actions give rise to the saying 'tender loving care'…?) This engine was hired on a total of six occasions between 1912 and 1922, by which time the hiring charge was £2 10s 0d per day. In 1923 the Great Western also tried to hire *Palmerston* again, but the Festiniog had to refuse due to its own motive power shortages. This picture shows *Palmerston* at the original Aberystwyth terminus with three coaches and a brake-van ready to leave for Devil's Bridge on 13 August 1913. *LCGB, Ken Nunn Collection*

Below Taken on the same date, by the looks of it a dull and windy summer's day, *Palmerston* is approaching Aberystwyth on a return journey from Devil's Bridge. *LCGB, Ken Nunn Collection*

During the weekend of 13/14th September 1986 there was another Festiniog visitor, this time the company's Alco-built 2-6-2T *Mountaineer*, accompanied by its driver Evan Davies. This photograph shows the engine climbing hard near Rheidol Falls on the 14th, and the view into the valley with 'the stag' prominent on the south-facing hillside. *HB*

71

Here is *Mountaineer* again on the last stages of its journey climbing towards Devil's Bridge with the 14.30 train from Aberystwyth on 13 September 1986. *HB*

It is only in recent times that a Rheidol engine has left its home territory. This interesting picture shows No 9 *Prince of Wales* working a 'Santa Special' towards Pontsticill on the Brecon Mountain Railway on 12 December 1992. The locomotive had been sent to the BMR workshops for repair and is being run in after overhaul before returning to Aberystwyth. Note that the tender of the BMR's *Graf Schwerin-Lowitz* is temporarily attached to No 9. *John K. Williams*

Rolling-stock

Above This picture well illustrates the two types of open wagons built for the railway. Seen outside the old loco shed in August 1967, nearest is Loco 34141, built by Midland Carriage & Wagon Co Ltd for the Plynlimon & Hafan Railway and sold to the Vale of Rheidol in 1901, where it became No 21. It has end-door opening. The second is branded ED and DW – something of an administrative 'overkill' as all the wagons were used indiscriminately for coal or ballast as and when required. No 34104 was built by Midland Carriage & Wagon in 1906 with side-door opening to become Vale of Rheidol No 4. The third wagon is another end-opening ex-Hafan. *Alan Wild*

Left Western Region No 8510 is one of the three ex-Hafan open wagons bought in 1901 (see above), and was converted into a bolster. The picture was taken at Aberystwyth on 3 June 1963. *John Edgington*

In 1938 the Great Western built three new guard's vans to replace the three originally supplied in 1902. They were 13 feet long with a wheel base of 6ft 6in, and numbered 135 to 137. No 135 was scrapped by the London Midland Region in 1968, and this photograph shows the two that survived, both looking woebegone and weather-beaten at Aberystwyth on 4 June 1963. No 136 was sold to the Welsh Highland Railway in 1980 and No 137 remains, now smartly repainted in chocolate and cream livery. *John Edgington*

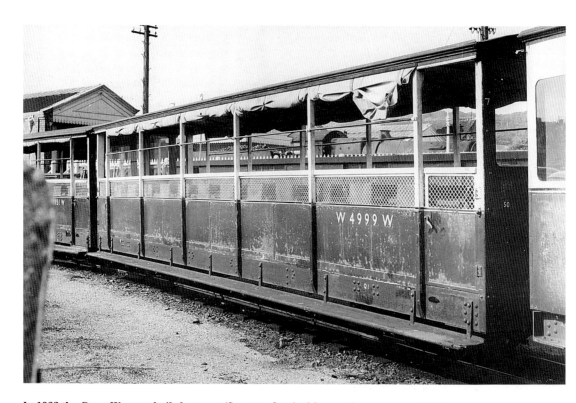

In 1923 the Great Western built four new 'Summer Cars' with a seating capacity of 48. There was a door at each corner and diamond-mesh safety panels above the waist, with a half canvas screen kept rolled up below the roof for use in inclement weather. Here W4999W is seen at Aberystwyth on 1 June 1963 in weathered condition, but 20 years later its fortunes had greatly improved – by 19 June 1983 it has been transformed into a 'Vista Car', the Wales Tourist Board and Development Board for Rural Wales jointly sponsored its conversion. An extra charge was made for travelling in it, and seating was arranged as two rows of upholstered seats facing across the valley, with passengers looking through large, deep viewing windows. It is seen here, less than two weeks after commissioning, with a rake of stock freshly repainted into the time-honoured Great Western chocolate and cream livery, all looking extremely smart. *John Edgington/HB*

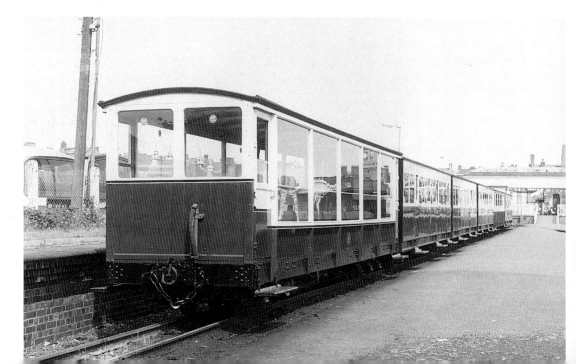

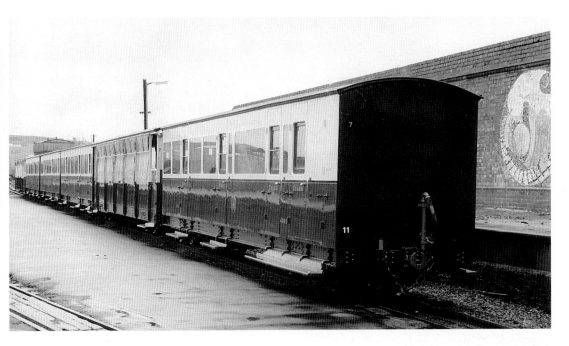

Above 1983 saw the return of the coaches to GWR chocolate and cream livery, and here are six at Aberystwyth station waiting to work to Devil's Bridge on the Spring Gala Day, 2 May. From right to left, they are 1st/3rd Brake 4995, 'Summer Car' 4149, 3rd 4147, 3rd 4994, 3rd 4143 and 'Summer Car' 4997. *HB*

Below A 1938-built 'Summer Car' in chocolate and cream livery with the Vale of Rheidol emblem in the centre panel – very smartly presented for the 2002 season. *HB*

Above A 1938-built 3rd Class coach, containing 48 seats accessed by three doors on each side. It was photographed at Aberystwyth in chocolate and cream livery with the Vale of Rheidol emblem on 5 May 2002. *HB*

Below The interior of 3rd Class coach No 6 in the formation of the 15.45 train from Devil's Bridge on 1 September 1998. The photograph shows the means of access; the seats are laid out as 16-seat bays at each end with one 24-seater bay in the middle. Seat backs are of course kept low so as to afford all passengers maximum visibility. *HB*

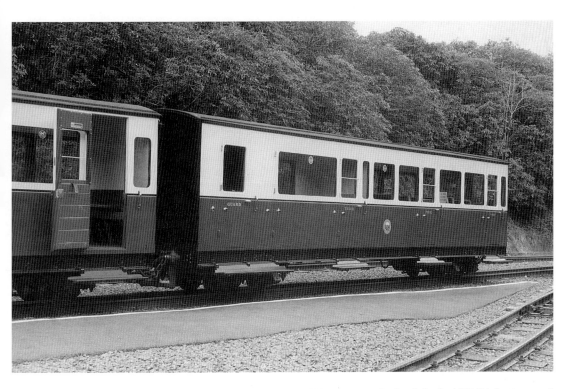

Above Of the batch of 12 new coaches built at Swindon in 1938, two were Brake 3rds. In 1983/84 the long end compartment in each was upholstered and carpeted and converted to 1st Class, thereby becoming 1st/3rd Brakes. This is No 11 seen at Devil's Bridge on 5 May 2002. *HB*

Below Two ex-South African 2-foot-gauge bogie hoppers were adapted for use as bogie ballast wagons in 2000/2001, and with a capacity of 17 tons they have proved a most useful asset. They were originally built in 1976 and worked on the Avontuur line in Cape Province, but are now numbered 33 and 34, and painted grey with black underframes and white-on-black markings. A Vale of Rheidol emblem is affixed near the body centre. *HB*

Two wagons built by Butterley for Bowaters' 2ft 6in-gauge line in Kent, and later sold to the railway at Whipsnade, were bought in 1995 for their bogies. These were re-gauged to 1ft 11½in, and rebuilt for use as rail-carrying vehicles. *HB*

INDEX